Femme Eterna

Praise for Femme Eterna

As Lyn Lifshin illuminates the lives of Enheduanna, Scheherazade, and Nefertiti, her poems also cast light on humanity's collective soul with lush references to the sensuality and the sharp mentalities of these three great feminine social forces. These are the people we all long to be—outspoken, courageous, personal, and political—three trailblazing comets across our historical skies. The drama of their accomplishments and their times, as poetically portrayed in *Femme Eterna*, comes together in Lifshin's inimitable and grandly classical style the way a strand of pearls creates a necklace to enhance any woman's natural and spiritual beauty.

— **Christina Zawadiwsky,** author of *The Hand On The Head Of Lazarus* and recipient of the National Endowment Award.

Lady Lyn empathizes so well with these three luminous women—Enheduanna, Scheherazade, and Nefertiti—that when she adopts each one as a persona, she almost becomes that woman whose life she is so closely examining. With compassion, she brings each woman's concerns, dreams, bravery, and experiences to life. Lifshin gives each of these women the kind of dimension that makes them seem to come into existence for her readers. By offering these particular women a spotlight, Lifshin shines her brilliant light on every woman.

— **Dr. Maura Gage Cavell,** Professor of English, Louisiana State University Eunice

Femme Eterna
Copyright © 2014 Lyn Lifshin
Paperback ISBN: 978-0-9840352-5-0

All rights reserved: except for the purpose of quoting brief passages for review, no part of this book may be reproduced or transmitted in any form or by any means, electronic or mechanical, including photocopying, recording, or by any information storage and retrieval system, without permission in writing from the publisher.

Cover art: Tracy McQueen
Cover Design & Layout: Steven Asmussen
Editing: Elizabeth Nichols
Copyediting: Cin Hochman of "100 Proof"

Glass Lyre Press, LLC
P.O. Box 2693
Glenview, IL 60026

www.GlassLyrePress.com

Femme Eterna
Enheduanna, Scheherazade & Nefertiti

Poems by
Lyn Lifshin

Introduction

Recently, a Russian painter, Luba Sterlikova, had the idea that we could collaborate—combine her paintings and my poems based on them—to explore some of the most interesting women in history. Although I had written about women in the past, from Eve to women in the less-distant past, she had paintings of Scheherazade, and thought that Nefertiti and Enheduanna—and several other women, like Eve, Devi, Pachamama, and the Celtic Bird Goddess—would be exciting to explore in poems and paintings.

That project did not materialize—we both had extremely busy schedules, other projects, and travel, and the expense of having a sample book produced, a requirement of the contest, was too formidable—but I became fascinated by the stories of these women, and in particular, how they survived with courage, daring, and grace.

Because I knew the least about Enheduanna, I started reading all I could about her. I loved the fact that she was not only the first woman who signed her name to what she had written, but that she was also a poet. Often, when asked to submit work on a certain theme, I become engrossed in the subject and write a series of poems, not one or two, as if I can't bear leaving my subject. It is like being in a new world with them. I can almost feel the heat of the Euphrates, the smell of olive groves she wandered through. I tried to imagine how she felt, as a woman, having men listen to her; wondering if they really were listening to what she said or just watching her shiny dark lips as she wrote on her lapis lazuli tablet. I was impressed, imagining the patience and time it must have taken to write with a stylus and in cuneiform. When I was in Turkey, I saw the intricacies of similar cuneiforms, and was even more amazed at Enheduanna's accomplishments. I imagine, if she were alive in our time, she would be a woman at the forefront, maybe a jazz singer scatting and, of course, with her own blog.

It was easy to identify with Scheherazade, another storyteller, whose imagination kept her alive. She had to have been one of the bravest women—risking death each night. Having found his first wife unfaithful, the Sultan decided he hated all women, and would marry and kill a new wife every day. I think how, under pressure, Scheherazade had to keep her cool and come up with a new story to entertain the Sultan every night, never knowing if she would survive until dawn. Her lips, smelling of roses, would not measure up to his unearthly intellectual and spiritual lust. I can imagine her using words like a belly dancer uses her body to lure and hypnotize. Her palms must have been damp as morning approached, so close to him she could smell his beard. And then her relief, walking backward, maybe, out of his chamber, happy for at least one more day to feel the sun on her long black hair.

Nefertiti was probably the most beautiful of these women, although all three of them were described, at various times and in various ways, as luminescent, brilliant, enlightened, glowing, and dazzling. Physically, it is Nefertiti whose name is most associated with classical, physical beauty: the bust of her that is most famous could compete with many of today's models. I feel a sadness about her. As a young adult, she often appeared in public with her husband, the king, and her daughters. She enjoyed unprecedented power as co-regent with her husband. I wondered, as I read about her, if she ever feared that somehow this wonderful state might vanish, might dissolve. That she would be abandoned by her husband and banished from her home. Were the others jealous of her power, her beauty? Did she think about what could be lost in a day? Did she wonder, imagine her body, her bones desecrated in antiquity? Or how she would be dressed in her sarcophagus? Could she have imagined that so many novels and poems would be written about her? Or that the granite heads, oils, and limestone reliefs would keep her image alive and glowing?

Contents

Enheduanna

In A Breeze Of Dates And Olives, 4000 Years BC	17
From Her Mother, The Sumerian	19
Years Before Jesus	21
Enheduanna	22
In The Shade Of Myrtle And Oak	23
I Think Of Enheduanna's Words	24
When The Moon Waxes, Then When The Moon Wanes	25
Enheduanna	26
Between The Euphrates And The Tigris	27
Enheduanna	28
Enheduanna's Dream #72	29
Some Days Her Heart Feels No Relief	30
Enheduanna	31
When I Think Of Enheduanna	33
While Everyone Else Is Still Sleeping	34
Sometimes Under The Last Raspberry Light	35
When She Pressed Her Web-Shaped Reed Into Soft Clay	36
When She Leans Into Her Dreams	37
Under Her Almond-Scented Braids	38
Imagining Enheduanna Singing Scat In A Karaoke Bar	39
As If Words Were Shapes	40
Enheduanna	41

I Think Of Enheduanna	42
Enheduanna	43
The Disk Of Enheduanna	44
Flamingos and Pelicans	46
Almost Like A Young Girl	47
Not Like Some Distant Abstract God, Not Like Some Terrible Scar	48
Some Mornings, Enheduanna Dresses In Flame	49
Enheduanna's Dream of Inanna	50
When The One You Love And Worship	51
Unlike Her Words, Her Blues Riff to Inanna	52
Enheduanna Creating Something That No One Has Before	53
Enheduanna On Inanna's Poems	54
Past Sacred Mountain And The Sacred Trees In The Desert	55
Enheduanna	56
Enheduanna, After Years in the Cove of the Temple	57
Because Inanna Is So Wild, So Beautiful	59
Round Blue Polished Beads Enheduanna Might Be Bored With	60
Who Knows If Enheduanna	61
Enheduanna	62
If She Had Known	63
When I Think Of Enheduanna	64
The Dream Image Of Enheduanna In The Sumerian Night	65
Her Eyes, Enormous	67

Scheherazade

Scheherazade's Journals	71
Under A Quilt Of Stars	72
Scheherazade	73
You Might Wonder	75
Scheherazade	76
How Could Her Palms Not Be Wet?	77
Scheherazade, As The Sun Goes Down	78
Scheherazade	79
Each Night She Is Like A Drowning Nymph	80
Scheherazade	81
I Think Of Her In Some Filmy Silk	82

Nefertiti

Nefertiti	87
She Slides	88
Exotic as the Nefer Beads	90
I Think Of Nerfertiti's Days Before Her Six Girls	92
Perpetual Arousal: She Dressed For Appeal	94
Nefertiti	95
Hours Posing for the Sculpture	97
Nefertiti Posing Hours with the Nile as a Backdrop	98
Afternoons, Alone in the Temple for Hours	100
Nefertiti on a Night She Couldn't Sleep	101
Sitting on Her Husband's Knees	102
When I Read How King Akhenaten's	103
Did the King Shudder, Knowing How Many Men Wanted Her	104

Nefertiti as America's Top Model	105
Nefertiti	107
Nefertiti	108
Nefertiti	109
While She Poses	110
Nefertiti	111
Think of Nefertiti	113
Why, Maybe, There is a Flaw in the Gorgeous Bust of Nefertiti	115
Those Days Posing for the Artist	117
How Nefertiti Got Her Blue-Black Hair and Disappeared	119
In One Shrine	120
Another Dead End	121
The Beautiful One Has Come	122

Enheduanna

I

Enheduanna was a high priestess in the Sumerian city-state of Ur. She was also the daughter of Sargon, founder of one of the first empires in human history. She lived from 2285-2250 BC, and became the first author—the first poet of either sex—to have signed her name to what she wrote: a collection of hymns written for forty-two temples throughout the southern half of ancient Mesopotamia, the Sumer civilization now known as Iraq.

I imagine her, a young woman sitting near the Nile in a wind of olives, praising the ancient deity Inanna and finding parallels to her own life in her hymns. Using a stylus made of woven grass, Enheduanna pressed the wedge-shaped reed into soft clay to write her songs, using cuneiform signs that had evolved from literal pictographs—signs that carried multiple meanings—and created poems that could be read with various interpretations, achieving the ambiguity that poetry demands. Reading her poems, the ancient world of Mesopotamia becomes less distant and foreign. You can almost smell the saffron, feel the hot dust near the pyramids.

The collected hymns became part of the literary canon of the remarkable Sumerian culture, and were copied by scribes in the temples for hundreds of years after Enheduanna's death. She continued to be remembered as an important figure, perhaps even attaining semi-divine status. Like the goddess Inanna, Enheduanna cries out and sings her own terrors and love in poems of darkness and rebirth. Her poems represent the first existing account of an individual's consciousness of her inner life, and reflect Enheduanna's own spiritual and psychological liberation from being an obedient daughter in the shadow of her ruler father to stepping out into her own life. Perhaps she was the very first feminist.

In A Breeze Of Dates And Olives, 4000 Years BC

In the shadow of a
white glowing house,
a young woman moves
thru reeds and barley.
Her hair shimmers in
the hot light like
ripples on the Euphrates.
In the distance, the
soft sounds of a
stringed instrument.
Children singing to the
Oud. She is Enheduanna,
daughter of Sargon.
Sun turns her copper breasts
fire. How can she know,
this man who brought her
berries in a clay dish
is not only the founder of
one of the first empires
in history, a reign that will
last long after his
daughter is no longer
stunned by the majesty's
terror and is wild
to carve her heart's
words, chisel stone with
her fierce passion, a
world grounded in
desire for gods and
goddesses, but is her father.
She feels braided to her life
with irresistible power
and ripeness. Birds no
one now living can
see dart thru brambles,

but Enheduanna hardly
sees them, already
humming, burning,
lost in the riffs of love,
carving her breath
and heartbeat into clay
tablets with a small knife
like a stylus that might
as well be part of her
body, seething and wild
to become the first writer
in recorded history to
sign her name to
what she wrote

From Her Mother, The Sumerian

history and religion, with
their goddesses and
temples more dazzling
than sunbeams with
lustrous lapis lazuli beads.
Enheduanna listened in
the glistening and fiery
light. Mornings before the
dew dissolves and goats
move in a wave of
hooves across the plains,
Enheduanna contemplates
the radiance of the
goddesses, imagines Inanna's
dazzling, irresistible
ripeness, radiant as perfectly
shaped fresh fruit. Some–
where else, someone is
shaping mud and reeds into
a house that will have its
own glow. Enheduanna,
years before Sappho, shivers,
feels her skin on the verge,
a gasp at the mystery of
breath, breathtaking as the
story she writes of creation
itself, how a temple platform
rises to split heaven and earth.
In such a parched land,
water is as magical to Enheduanna
as the heat of a lover's tongue,
as startling as his fingers. She
hears stories of a sweet-water ocean,
the Abzu, with earth floating on
top. She is holding her sharpened

reed pen, bending into clay
as a breeze blows from
the Tigris, catches dry petals
as if they were butterflies
and sends them west,
while Enheduanna forgets to
eat, so wild to praise
Inanna, the amazing goddess
who gave birth to all life from
her water, that life emerging from
teeming waters, her heavenly womb,
and Enheduanna, bursting with
passion, stamps the clay
cuneiform, signs her name, as
no one ever had

Years Before Jesus

Sargon must have held
this baby daughter,
date palm fronds
blowing in an olive
wind. His pale jewel.
Lutes in the distance,
small stringed
instruments. Under
the house, bones
of dead families
wrapped in maps and
carpets, dead children
in clay jars with
precious objects: cow,
lamb, turtles, jars
of rich food
and barley, with the
hope that the
spirit may be re-
born, come back to
them in the flesh again

Enheduanna

The first poet whose
name we know, there
under palm leaves
with her tablet of
lapis lazuli, deep as
her eyes. A true woman
in the shade of the
holy potash plant,
moving like a young
cat. The goddess
of writing, learning,
the harvest. "My king,"
she almost sang,
"something has been
created that no one has
created before." The
light must have had a
tangerine cast to it,
ribbons of sun braiding
with the onyx hair
of Enheduanna, a
shrine in a pure place

In The Shade Of Myrtle And Oak

in the light, dusky
as olive branches,
Enheduanna twists
her long hair into
loops of jasper
and onyx, hair
ribbons of gold
leaf. On her wrist,
lapis lazuli and
agates. When she
moves thru night,
her multi-chain
of carnelian and
ivory, anklets
of silver darting
thru darkness
like stars

I Think Of Enheduanna's Words

in the fruit of
date palm trees

just out of reach.
Stone will hold

her words long
after the dates

bloom for ages,
beckon like

the trees in the
scorching summer

wind. They seem,
like her words—

precious

When The Moon Waxes, Then When The Moon Wanes

Enheduanna played
the afternoon shadows
like a piano, a harp
made for a pocket
of air like a singer
belting the blues.
She chiseled words
in clay, sucked up
from each equinox.
For the solstices,
metal and copper
anklets, love rings,
exotic weavings
from *anki*, the
Sumerian word for
the universe, which
refers to their god
of the sky

Enheduanna

    Ornament of the
    house and sky. Emerald
    vines sprout from
    her forehead
    and temples. In
    a dream, she smiles
    slightly. Her eyelids
    pale blue, iridescent as
    the blue petals that
    open as the
    green leaves grow
    toward heaven,
    flowers under earth
    so long they can't
    help but break
    free, pulsing, alive,
    luminous in darkness
    as Enheduanna's
    poems, her words,
    intense as those flowers

Between The Euphrates And The Tigris

when stars still
dribbled light
on the sand,
before dawn,
she lets her
hair unravel,
the rose she
carries drops its
petals. Will
she dance with
the god of
the moon?
Early before
wet clay
hardens, she
presses the
stylus, gives
birth to what
explodes from
her heart

Enheduanna

A last light
leaves slashes of
scarlet ribbon

She can't let
the day go, she
is obsessed,

she is carrying
the embryo of a
poem in her fingers

Soon it will
be dark, but while
the temples are

blazing, as if the
light came from
the crude clay

bricks, she can't
stop pressing
clay as if

each word,
each image,
were exorcism

Enheduanna's Dream #72

something skitters in
the palm trees, then
slithers thru reeds, but
Enheduanna is in a
dream, is in the zone.
She is spinning words
to the goddess who
carried ruined roses,
woven across many
centuries, to stand
against the ransacking
of sacred places. Sky
goes raspberry, color of
Enheduanna's lips;
still she's lost in her own
lush words, an amalgam
of poetry, howls, and
jazz, praising the
goddess' brilliance
that melts two suns and
a full moon that dips
to earth like fine oil

Some Days Her Heart Feels No Relief

The grape arbor
feels like exile.
Stars, chunks
of ice. She won't
be taboo in spite
of rage and pain.
"Under her
tasseled shawl,
her heart bangs."
Her eyes make
holes in the
afternoon light,
eyes startling
as lapis lazuli.
Can you still be
a poet-priestess
when your skin
wants a flesh man?

Enheduanna

    listened to stories of
her father's journey
from Kish, how the
camels lurched
toward the temple
of the Moon God.
Desert flowers dot
the pale sand. She
braids the stories of
Grandfather, brought
up by a water-thrower,
a magician, god of
sweet waters,
wisdom. I think of
her, a young woman,
maybe dreaming of
boys, carving her
passion, her terror,
and love into shapes
in clay, in awe of
strong, beautiful
goddesses but especially
Inanna, who glows like
a jewel, a crystal ball
Enheduanna nearly
can see herself
in, a mirror thru which she can
almost tell what's
ahead for her. Her
skin still smooth and
clear. I think of
her probably not even
knowing she is
the first author in
world literature to

sign her name to what
she has written. A
young girl in sandals
and a sash of woven
grape leaves, carrying
in the morning light
a masterpiece, vivid,
glistening, still damp,
and the clay braiding
rhetoric, structure, and
sacred testimony,
with clues about her
creative process 2000
years before Homer

When I Think Of Enheduanna

I imagine flowers and
vines sprouting from
her hair, green vines
in a dream where her
brain sends pale
flowers and moons
and fish and all-seeing
eyes up into the sky.
I think of her skin
under pale cotton in
the July sun, her words
green as the flowers
and lilies she prayed
would thrive, and they
did. To some, she was
the most important
religious figure of the
day, but I think of her
hand warming as she
clutched her tablet of
lapis lazuli, half wonder-
ing if she wasn't just too
young to be entrusted
with all this

While Everyone Else Is Still Sleeping

Enheduanna braids her
long black hair. Behind
her eyes, temples grow
out of cosmic mist,
lift their necks to the sky.
Sometimes she longs
to be small enough
to play in her mother's
quilts and weavings.
Sometimes she feels over-
whelmed by life's mystery
and fear, its terror and
dread, its beauty and
desire. Think of her as a
torch singer, belting
out what scorches and
what can calm, her songs
carved into hard clay that
will dance, a wild jazz
scat. Her skin smells of
saffron and sun; the music
of the Euphrates in the
background, she scatters
her stories in the rushes.
Images flutter in and
out of the palace walls until,
like an ink tattoo, she
pierces the clay like skin
and tells the wild story

Sometimes Under The Last Raspberry Light

Enheduanna drifts into
stories of the Grain Goddess,
sister of the Cattle Goddess.
She half dreams of dark
caves before they knew
how to eat bread. Dates
drop to the pale sand. She
fingers her woven red
threads, can imagine dark
sun on bodies that knew
nothing of clothes. She's
lost in the myths, the tales
of a wonderful balsa
flowing from a goddess
whose face was radiance
adorned with precious stone.
In her lap, a green lion with
blood flowing from his
side. She was crowned with
a diadem and set as a star
in the highest heaven

When She Pressed Her Web-Shaped Reed Into Soft Clay

it was as if the words
and symbols were
fingers, each shape
glowing with the
ambiguity poetry
demands. Her arms,
saffron-perfumed, her
hair in a clasp of
reeds. Could she
have dreamt
her explosion of
words, layers on top
of layers, the bottom
images showing thru
like pentimento
in art, where
images painted
over another one
eventually seep
thru; would, 500 years
later, stun and
astonish, intense as
the scarlet bird in the
date tree. In her own
spell, Enheduanna
braided her life with
the goddess Inanna. She
signed her own
name to what could
have been a torch
burning, the first poet
to do so, as if she'd
had a choice

When She Leans Into Her Dreams

When she's the instrument of
a song to Inanna. When she
doesn't know how to be
calm and the reeds
and shimmery winged
things keep dancing. When
she fears mountain
water will turn to ash. When
she pleads to the one who
wraps her heart in
evening's scarlet ashes and
plays the evening rain
like a sacred heart.
Enheduanna, her anklet of
lapis lazuli playing its
own riff, her father,
the king's, voice in her
ear like thunder, when she
stamps in clay her
prayers, her loyalty, her respect
for those who make earth
beautiful all on their
own. She writes of their
powers over desire, writes
of flowers, joy, of the
stars and the sea
and its dark waters

Under Her Almond-Scented Braids

under dust wind in the
palm trees, Enheduanna
mingles her life with
the goddess she is
obsessed with. Both are
wild and beautiful,
powerful, clever, and
ready to fly thru
the universe, a cyclone,
tsunami. Fierce as
dragons or tigers, each
dreams the terror of
being stripped of power.
Inanna's blood mixes
with her blood to give
birth to her song.
Stripped of everything
except the creation born of
an empty page, her skin
on the skin of stone,
holding, breathing rules,
making images as
astonishingly beautiful as
Inanna, she is wild to
go where no one has come
back from, in her flowing
red robe, necklace of
lapis, and carnelian vest,
pleased with what
she made, to what she
brought forth, like
any birth, so she signed
her name

Imagining Enheduanna Singing Scat In A Karaoke Bar

showing off her new ink.
Let her father do what
he has to, being leader,
in control, doing his
kingly duties. Today no
woman is as wildly
passionate, a headstrong
beauty, a lyrical torch
singer, who would be as
happy not being out
with the crowds.
Ambivalent and fearsome,
her voice a jazz blues
riff, feminist jazz
humming. And would
you expect any less from
a woman who couldn't
sleep and walked out alone
under the stars and could
not keep what was
pulsing inside her, dug
her feelings into clay
and signed her name?

As If Words Were Shapes

you could finger and touch,
Enheduanna's skin soothes
and varnishes the passion
seething inside her. It's not
enough to be the daughter
of a king and sit calmly in
the castle when what burns
inside her howls for a way
out. It's not enough to learn
history as it happens, not
enough to be the first woman
to hold the title of *En*, for
high priestess, early spouse
of a deity. Not enough
to be fed exotic fruits and
plum wine, have dates
on glistening platters and
shawls of scarlet and soft blue
wool, when all that matters
is that she save Inanna,
that her tears and verbs and
weeping, her moaning
and prayers keep her strong,
so Inanna can be strong
and beautiful and
hold Enheduanna in the
cove of love

Enheduanna

no one else had ever
written about them-
selves or their feelings
about the deities.
Mornings in the
shade of the palms,
lost in her new poems
to the goddess Inanna,
lost in the passion,
the terror, and love
for one she sees her-
self in so clearly.
Maybe in the shadow
sculpture of Inanna,
before clay became
fragments and her
long braids dusk,
she shivered, sensed
these golden mornings
couldn't stay. But, for the
moment, every inch
of her sings the great
news of Inanna, a chant,
a hymn, where she
promises she is hers.
"My Lady, I will
proclaim your great
news and your glory,"
and beg as doves and
desert bees fill the
clean air, Inanna's
"heart cool off for me."

I Think Of Enheduanna

rising from the couch
of dream divination.
I can imagine her
wondering, not
sure she wants this
role as priestess,
wanting to walk
among the blue
flowers lost in day-
dreams, a boy she has
a crush on. Maybe
she wonders why she
can't live like an
ordinary girl, not
follow her father's
orders. Why should
she have to write
to secure her family's
hold on the country he
took over? Sure, she
speaks the Sumerian
tongue, but why does
she have to have
this burden? Maybe
she watches the
desert birds become
black specks in
the tangerine sky and
longs for their freedom,
years before she'd
understand she was
her own person and
would discover her
inner values, and exalt
them as knowledge
and wisdom, as
law and faith
and joy

Enheduanna

Before sun scorches brick
and date palms, she lets
the almond wind warm
her hair. Her poet's beauty is
in the ordinary, catching
what glistens. She dares
to imagine what is behind
human sight and knowledge
on a stone tablet. Soap
and water for ritual
cleansing. "Why is life
so full of hardship?" she
sighs, pressing precious
oil from a tough, unyielding
hill of barley, praying to
all creation that what
she writes will be as
alive as her skin

The Disk Of Enheduanna

After a long trip, after the canals
between the Euphrates and the
Tigris. After she was chosen
by the Moon God to be his
human wife, Enheduanna got
her name. Before she was
chosen, while reeds were
shaking in a wind of lilies and
almonds, renowned seers read the
stars, extracted the liver from a
spotless sheep to check the
slim, long-haired girl, to predict
her worth from intricate shapes,
hills and valleys to see if she
were the one, the star of harvests,
fertility, queen of animals,
and the wealth and happiness
of all human subjects. Then
Enheduanna inscribed, in her
own handwriting, on the back of
an alabaster disk, that she was
the true Lady of Nanna, never
imagining that thousands of years
later someone would find
that alabaster broken into pieces,
her text in fragments but, luckily,
copied by a scribe in the old
Babylonian period, 500 years
after her birth. Depicted as the
moon in front of a stepped edifice,
she walks with robed, clean-shaven
priests. One carries a drink from
the altar; the other, a frond or
sprinkler; and the last, a pocket.
She wears a floral robe, a

thick headband, with her long
hair falling down the back and in
braids down the side of her face,
calm and beautiful—you can
only imagine her dreams
and wild yearnings

Flamingos and Pelicans

outside the palace,
on the way to Siberia,
to Africa, teals and
reeds and warblers
seem code for
Inanna. Enheduanna
rubs night from her
eyes. The Sacred Ibis
and African Darter
sing of a strange wind
no light can grow
in. Nothing like the
sun Inanna threw out
like dandelions,
skimming over chaos
in her wild red hair

Almost Like A Young Girl

with a crush on an older
woman, or a child idolizing
a big sister, Enheduanna's
astonishment, devotion
to Inanna, can hardly be
contained. You can feel
your skin prickle, as hers
surely did, wanting to cage
and store a moment of
grace, still entranced by a
goddess so good at being
reckless. Even before it's
bright, Enheduanna
half tastes the scents of
the fig trees, remembers
dreams of being transformed
to trees. You might think
there were glass balls
in her fingers, that she knew
Daphne had turned into a pine
tree, a laurel, a yew. She
calls Inanna *sister*, wants some
artist to make her a soothing
brew for this spirit who
comes from the place of palm
trees and sweet melons,
from the place full of saffron
and fragrant oils, and begs
her, the one who knows the
mystery of birds, whispers in
red grass for them to come to
quiet her shattered soul

Not Like Some Distant Abstract God, Not Like Some Terrible Scar

For Enheduanna, devoted to
capturing the lush Rose of
Jericho, with its rolled-into-a-
tight-ball curves, as some nights
she feels, and then so like
certain terrors in the wake of
Inanna's blessing, like the
plant she breaks loose from
its root, her skin fluttering.
They enter the sweet heat and
then, until rain falls, plant
branches that uncurl to protect
the center of the plant that
could be her heart. She waits for
Inanna, waits for seeds to
generate long new roses
to grow white as snow she
may never see, but will
note in her hymn to Inanna,
hopes her gorgeous song
will melt moon and stars
and drip on to earth
like the rose balm

Some Mornings, Enheduanna Dresses In Flame

    like Inanna, clutching
    longing like the
    sharpened reed she
    will plunge into
    clay. Years before
    feminist appears on
    anyone's lips, she
    is flying under long
    hair, danger braiding
    the rain, wild to
    appease Inanna, bring
    her laughter and
    light, a cove
    she can thrive in,
    like marshes in the
    desert, reaping
    gold petals

Enheduanna's Dream of Inanna

How she tosses her hair,
brings sun like yellow
dandelions out of a
basket. How can
Enheduanna sleep,
longing for Inanna's
safety. Only a goddess
knows the arts of
giving birth and the
healing and magical
medicinal powers.
Only they have power
over desire, flowers,
stars and the sky,
and dark waters. Only
the goddess truly
knows the cycle of
life and death; only
Inanna, always a mystery,
spitting poison, brings
forth flowers, the
brightest stars and lilies.
Enheduanna plucks
stalks of Puschkinia, the
blue-white flowers,
feels she is like the
plant, tolerating drought,
waiting and waiting

When The One You Love And Worship

is like a sister, not
a faceless, voiceless
wonder. When even
July birds dissolve
in pale heat and
the temple gold blurs.
The people go in-
side to worship at
their private altars,
receive prayers
as they twist
and untwist strands
of sadness and
light as a date palm
in the fruit wind
dangles dark globes
in bunches until,
like prayers, what's
longed for is
harvested

Unlike Her Words, Her Blues Riff to Inanna

sealed in clay, recited
500 years and then
resurrected almost
6,000 years later. Her
jewels untouched for
years and years.
People who knew
where treasures were
had been slaughtered
or taken captive,
never to return to their
houses. The secrets
of the jewels' location
died with them, like
what Enheduanna
dreamed nights, going
to sleep with the
night birds and sand
birds in the tamarisk
poplars and licorice,
close to the music of
the Tigris
and Euphrates

Enheduanna Creating Something That No One Has Before

for those who want her
more down to earth,
more sensual, flesh
and hair you can
run your fingers thru,
think how she advises
when servants let the
flocks loose, when
cattle and sheep are
returned to their pens.
Then Enheduanna,
like the nameless poor,
wears only a simple
garment, the pearls of
a prostitute are placed
around your neck
and you are likely to
snatch a man from the
tavern, then hurry
to the cattle, where 7
nymphs share the
bed with you

Enheduanna On Inanna's Poems

    she can turn a
    man into a woman,
    a woman into a
    man, make any-
    one desirable.
    Gain, profit, and
    great wealth
    and success are
    at her mercy. She
    can make men
    virile, send
    guardian
    angels, but if
    you displease her,
    that's another
    story

Past Sacred Mountain And The Sacred Trees In The Desert

wild fruit trees Enheduanna's
headdress will mirror, with
its cluster of gold pomegranates
and fruits hanging together,
shielded by their leaves
as she is shielded by her poems,
their wild praise for Inanna.
Gold stems and fruit on pods of
gold and carnelian. Enheduanna
hears redbirds in willow branches.
Before night-water is licked
from all the leaves, she drifts
in poems of love for Inanna. In the
myth, the mystery of what
Inanna could be thinking, in the
Sycamore, a clue to the sun in her
eyes, the shudder at someone
who, like Innana, visits the world of
the dead and still returns. Enheduanna
wraps the green leaves closer,
strokes the Ished, a fruit-bearing tree
that loves only the waters of certain
rivers. She shakes, wonders who will
want her, gray as dusk, dark
as the tree that returns the dead
person to the Sycamore wood

Enheduanna

mysterious as the
taste of fruit no
longer growing.
Years from when
she picks Wild
Iris and the wild
flower she uses
for bathing, she
walks thru Joshua
trees and dark
blue thistle

Enheduanna, After Years in the Cove of the Temple

in the stillness of
stories of wars and
love and music,
easy in the green
wind of dates and
clay jewels. Night
birds and then,
suddenly, like a
hawk pouncing on
doves, she is exiled
from the temple.
Dark blue in the
haze, in the
bread. Everything
ransacked. Now
Enheduanna is being
raped, left to
wander the hills.
Everything rose
and gold is
smashed, every-
thing living that
can't still be
what it was,
abandoned, with
no one to help,
as far as she
could be from the
ones who once
protected her,
she calls out
Inanna, wild for
the goddess'

epic journey to the
Land of No Return
to soothe her
own banishment
from power

Because Inanna Is So Wild, So Beautiful

because she is famous
in the stars, in the
earth, in the earth's
clay and flowers,
and fearless enough
to hurl herself over the
hills like a dragon,
abandon everything
to see what it is,
like in the Netherworld,
in the Land of No
Return. When
Enheduanna writes
about the terrors, the
horrors, she mingles her
life with Inanna's. No
one else's life
parallels hers so vividly.
Both stripped of
their powers, left ruined
and helpless in the
hands of their enemies,
like diamonds and emeralds
smothered in mud

Round Blue Polished Beads Enheduanna Might Be Bored With

    and dark copper
    shells might follow
    Enheduanna into
    her tomb: metal,
    petals, a tiara
    of gold, polished
    beads. Can she
    imagine her jewels
    and gold rosettes
    mingled with
    dried bone? The
    gold hairnet tangled
    with her own
    burnished hair?
    Will she dream
    what is, even as it
    presses her skin,
    astonishes, priceless
    as gold diadems
    embellished
    with blue, green, red
    and white enameled
    flowers; will, at
    her death, be
    untouched for years,
    never return to
    her home?

Who Knows If Enheduanna

created autumn and
winter 4,000 years
ago. Who can ever
be sure how to
translate anything
from a 4,000-year-old
dead language written
in cuneiform with-
out even a Rosetta
Stone artifact that
relates cuneiform
to a language like
Hebrew? But when
these texts are
long and not very
simple, are there
really enough artifacts
with a broad enough
vocabulary to
decipher a text?

Enheduanna

Was it her passion? Her
lips, dark as pomegranates,
that made men listen?
Or how she opened
her mouth, luminous as
her tablet of lapis lazuli
reflecting the sky,
soothed the frazzled
and lonely? You can see
her in a field of potash
and stylus reeds, born to
teach and delight

If She Had Known

she would be remembered
as the earliest known
poet. And if she knew
hymns to Inanna would be
praised as the first to use
a first-person narrative,
would she have changed a
word? Been less mysterious?
Written more about being
the wife of the Moon God,
Nanna? Told us more
of her father, Sargon?
Written more about her
mother's dreams and fears?
Written with the same
gut-ripping honesty?
And tell how, in the palace,
she pulled from her heart
and blood, such as some
say, "psychological,
sophisticated insights that
made her a sheer genius,
unparalleled even by
Shakespeare."

When I Think Of Enheduanna

loosening her hair,
then binding her hair.
And the way she turned
chaos into cosmos.
Long, dark strands,
like the goddess'
nets and knots. I can
imagine the sweet
wind of dates blowing
thru the reeds, her
skin tawny, her
mind racing, wild to
make and capture
a woman's suffering
and redemption
in words so close to
flesh you can imagine
the verbs turned
flesh, see how, in the
Sumerian language,
the word for
woman
and the
word for *enchantment*
are the same

The Dream Image Of Enheduanna In The Sumerian Night

smelling of olives
and dates and oil.
Stars rest on her
eyelids, her skin
luminous, color
of sand under a
full moon. She
could be dream-
ing of Inanna: her
fierceness, her
beauty. Behind
eyelashes thicker
than ferns, she is
wild for Inanna's
healing touch.
Vines sprout
from her cheek-
bones against
a black sky, her
forehead a green
maze of what
grows. Pale hills,
ivory shadows,
and a milky sliver
moon. So much
that's green as
the words and
images left in clay
of Enheduanna's
passion, words
that glow from
4,000 BC, still
palpable as skin

or a glistening
orange or blue
and fawn flowers,
symbols, shapes
that, as Sappho
wrote later, "some-
one, I tell you,
will remember us."

Her Eyes, Enormous

burning coal. From her
temple, Enheduanna
watched the stars, the
moon, the mover of
lights in the black velvet
seas. In one sculpture,
her eyes tear a hole in you,
kohl rims a fiery glare.
Words and symbols
pressed into glass 500
years after she died

Scheherazade

II

Against her father's wishes, Scheherazade dared to volunteer to spend the night with King Shahryar. Betrayed by his first wife, the king was intent on marrying as many virgins as possible, then killing them in the morning, in his ongoing anger at his first wife's infidelity. By the time Scheherazade volunteered, he had already killed one thousand women, beheading them in the early morning after an amorous wedding night. Before she began this dangerous adventure, Scheherazade had read over a thousand books of geography and history, and spent days researching the legends of earlier kings.

She studied Philosophy and Science and books of poetry until she knew the poems by heart. That night, the king lay awake and listened, mesmerized, as Scheherazade told her story. She stopped in the middle and asked the king if she might please say goodbye to her beloved sister. The king agreed, then asked her to finish the story, but Scheherazade said there was no time, that it was dawn. So the king spared her life one day more so that she could finish. The next night, she finished, and began an even more exciting tale and, again, stopped halfway through. Each night, the stories became more entrancing and so the king kept Scheherazade alive for one thousand nights and one thousand stories. By the time she told him she had no more tales, the king had fallen in love. King Shahryar made Scheherazade his queen, and she made him a wiser and kinder man. They eventually had three sons.

Scheherazade's Journals

written in code only
her sister can read
if she doesn't make
it thru another night.
Who knows if his
body crushing hers
will be for sex or
death. She writes a
note to the ones she
could be leaving.
One dull story and
everything ends.
Her beauty, plum
nipples, her lips
smelling of roses
won't be enough if
the lure of her plots
and stories can't
measure up to his
unearthly intellectual
and spiritual lust

Under A Quilt Of Stars

like black onyx velvet.
She pulls, like someone
spinning straw into gold,
visions that stun, would
pull any man close, his
breath held, frozen. Her
stories, pungent as a
mango grove, intoxicating
as May wine in a night
garden of jasmine
and patchouli, lasso
your blood and
your dreams. Each plot
stuns and slithers in-
to a new one like
jeweled glass, ruby,
emerald, and sapphire
shards in a kaleidoscope.
She is enchanting,
gives you what you
can't let go of. A
magician, she is not
like a tree where the roots
have to end somewhere,
but is daring and
clever, wily as Coyote,
definitely not like those
afflicted at birth
with some
presentiment of loss

Scheherazade

Naturally, she'll be in blue,
not the wild bullfight flame
color that drives men wild,
as the story goes, but calm,
hypnotic, a frozen lake
spell that swirls men into
her words, a tornado
spinning, about to touch
down. She knows the ritual.
Her voice a lasso, a swirl, a
lariat. Her eyes, words, voice
hog-tie your breath. She is a
wild magnet; everything in
you is iron filings, unable
to resist. She will tell you
the dream where you feel your
skin pulled past deserts in
Tripoli, flung into an emerald-
studded tent, where whatever
you lusted for is pulled
from the lake behind her
eyes and the new moon of her
whispers turns darkness wild as
overflowing rivers in a tsunami.
It gets late, later, and no one
can sleep. Night's glistening
onyx. She is cunning, cat-
like. She is the horses running
until they forget they are
horses. Just as you think maybe
you've got her for good, have
her body where you want
it, light slices the room in two.
If you weren't so drunk on
her, you'd see her slight sneer,

how she catches her breath:
alive for one more day. How
she sees your longing, prays you
will never get used to it

You Might Wonder

even before being captive,
was she too often living
on the edge? Addicted
to danger? Was the
edge all she ever knew?
The intensity? Was it a
high to escape the knife
one more time? Never
feeling as alive? Does
she find him more
terrifying or more
seductive? Imagine
the velvet cushion, her
pale throat so close
to his knife and hands.
Was he so close
she could smell his
beard? Was the air too
still as clouds
covered the moon?

Scheherazade

She wants you
to be inconsolable,
wants you to keep
wanting more.
Somewhere under
her hair, wild plots
explode like kudzu,
covering a whole
house overnight. Her
stories grow like
an invasive species
taking root, taking
over. She'll reveal
just enough. Her
stories could be
a dance of veils,
hypnotic; her words,
a belly dancer's skin,
mesmerizing as car
lights you are the
frozen deer in
the trance of until
it's too late to
do her in

How Could Her Palms Not Be Wet?

Scheherazade, her
heart wild under silk.
I think of her when
the sky gets light,
fighting sleep, driven
to map out the next
night's plot. Each tale,
like the third person
in this ménage à
trois, where words
tempt more than bodies,
hair, and skin. She
knows, like a lover
who prays to never be
boring, her stories
must charm and
disarm, or she won't
be there to tell them

Scheherazade, As The Sun Goes Down

Maybe she thought of him
as a child asking to be told
about a past dream, or some
familiar story never ending
as it did. She knows his
tantrums, the knives in his
eyes. Others haven't made it,
escaped, stayed alive. But
she's got a stone-strong,
wild, riveting plot. No, *plots*,
and images to keep him as
glued to her as if she were
stripping, revealing slices
and flashes of an exotic, sexy
body. She's a quick-change
artist, her stories the cape the
bull of his appetite tries to
gore. There are bodies stock-
piled before her. She is steely,
fanatically bright. Their
nights are brilliant blue. Like
a magical tree's never-
ending explosion of plums,
she spins stories he can't help
but lust for more of, each
one more tantalizing

Scheherazade

How it was late, was
getting later. She
was walking a tight-
rope, couldn't know
if each story could
be the last. Adrenaline
pulses through this
chameleon. She's
wily as the Lorelei,
tempting and luring,
her words a mirage,
her only ammunition

Each Night She Is Like A Drowning Nymph

Like a woman pulled
out of the river
and dressed in warm
clothes, her lips
parted. The twist of
words that will
keep blood flowing
thru her body.
She could be a woman
close to drowning,
reeled in with eels and
seaweed, fins, like
Rapunzel shimmying to
freedom; her own
hair, her words,
a rope to escape

Scheherazade

    if she were to tell
her own story, if
she were to spin
images and verbs
of her nights, it
would never be
boring, would
never end. Like the
most skillful lover,
her nights are
never dull. Like
any woman who
has to do what
she has to do to
save her own life,
she had to keep
doing it, one
night at a time

I Think Of Her In Some Filmy Silk

    her skin rubbed
    with jasmine. Before
    the stars are rhinestones
    above the castle where
    he will enter her
    for what she knows
    could be the last time.
    The erotic and the
    life-threatening, a sash
    he could at any time
    undo, wrap too tight
    across her neck.
    Call her Wily Coyote.
    Everything is a trick.
    Who can imagine
    the names she
    calls him where he
    can't see her shuddering,
    as she lists the names
    of flowers that only
    open once

Nefertiti

III

Nefertiti is probably the most recognized of these three women and better known than her husband, King Akhenaten. Even in the ancient world, her beauty was famous, and the beautiful statue found in a sculptor's workshop is one of the most recognizable icons of ancient Egypt. She was more than a pretty face, however. She seems to have taken on an amazing level of importance and is depicted nearly twice as often in artwork than her husband, and once, even in the conventional pose of a pharaoh conqueror.

No one knows for sure if Nefertiti was of royal blood or whether she was the daughter of an army officer. We know that Nefertiti and the king had six daughters. We see many images of the king and queen inseparable in early panels, often with their daughters, in loving, almost utopian compositions. The king is shown riding with her in a chariot, kissing her in public, often sitting on his knees. At the corners of his granite sarcophagus, the place of honor usually given to famous deities, the king had statues of Nefertiti carved to protect his mummy.

We see her in beautiful clothes—a clingy robe tied with a red sash and a Nubian wig and with a queen's tri-partial wig. Sometimes she wears a crown with double plumes and a disk. She dressed for appeal, and part of this responsibility would have been to maintain a state of perpetual arousal. Some note her sweet voice and fair hands. At other times, she wore a mortar-shaped hat, in her leonine aspect as a sphinx.

Suddenly, Nefertiti disappeared from historical Egyptian records. Some thought she fell out of favor with the king, but others dismiss that. It is possible she died around the age of thirty. Some think she was a co-agent in disguise. Some think she even served as king after the death of Akhenaten. The mysteries only make her more intriguing.

She is best known for the limestone bust that many think is one of the greatest works of art in the pre-modern world. When it was found, there was a hush as they dusted years of debris to reveal her lips, full and a brilliant red, her eyelids and brows kohl. The bust shows her long, elegant neck, brightly colored beads against her tawny skin. Only an ear is missing and the color in one eye. Another mystery to excite the world's imagination.

Nefertiti

I imagine her sliding
silk over her
perfect arms, the
Egyptian sun's mouth
even at dawn
moving over her,
licking her
tawny skin. Beads
circle her long neck
as who knows
how many ardent
worshippers dream
their fingers might do,
wake up shaking
with fear and
desire. Eyes like no
other eyes, not
even Elizabeth Taylor's,
mahogany jewels,
hypnotic, entrancing,
a gaze so intense
no one needs
to tell you, as her
name itself
does, *the
beautiful one*

She Slides

    green silk over
    her bronze, almost
    golden body. Hot
    Egyptian light.
    How could she
    know that, years later,
    young girls would
    put necklaces on
    her statue, lightly
    scented candles
    and incense. Or
    worry, breaking
    the snake off a
    model of Tut's head-
    dress, that they
    will get a mummy
    curse. I think of
    Nefertiti, a pale
    yellow sky beyond
    the palace, pyramids
    reflected in still
    pools by dawn. She
    watches the night
    sand begin to
    glow, the lavender
    shadows, twists
    her ebony river of
    hair into carved
    tortoise shell combs,
    studded with
    alabaster. Near the
    canopied bed,
    eyes as gorgeous,
    if not as exquisite
    as hers, the cat

she knows, since
cats dream in
Egypt, has visions
she will, as the
day unfolds,
try to guess

Exotic as the Nefer Beads

elongated, exquisite, gold

no one is sure where
she came from.
A foreign princess,
15, hardly more than
a child, marrying a
king just a year later.
I think of her fastening
her bridal gown, that
at least she was not
a sacrifice like other
young virgins. Did she,
I wonder, look ahead,
imagine six daughters?
Imagine, as some
suppose, a son who
would later rule? She
could never have, I
bet, supposed many
would believe she was
that son, that boy, that
she would dress as
a man and rule when
others thought she had
disappeared or maybe
was murdered. Light
on the Nile, the pale
roses against a stubble
sky. How little there
to hint at what was
ahead; only her beauty,
her full lips the sculptor
caught, enhanced by
bold red eyelids and

brow outlined in black,
dark as the mysteries
surrounding her

I Think Of Nerfertiti's Days Before Her Six Girls

      gold circling her body,
      plentiful as the lush
      palms, the river of
      gold, silver, and
      turquoise fish. Did she
      feel lucky, a man who
      loved but also respected
      her, included women
      as he ruled? The
      sky, cloudless, this time
      of no war, smooth
      as her skin and
      the silk wrapping her
      gorgeous body, a
      freeze-frame of beauty.
      Her swan-like neck,
      eyes even Elizabeth Taylor
      would have yearned for.
      Poets wrote her praises
      on papyrus, played
      songs to her on
      mahogany lutes. Ivory
      statues of her favorite cats
      gleamed in the light.
      Wine no one can still
      imagine the taste of
      on her lips, she waited
      for her babies in the
      glow of the hot Egyptian
      light. Grapes, figs,
      and dates in a silver bowl,
      tubers, leaves, and
      seeds in a basket of

copper, she spent afternoons
boating, nights of music
and board games,
long before she had to
write letters to the
dead, and what was to
unroll started
unrolling

Perpetual Arousal: She Dressed For Appeal

someone says, and if she
fulfilled a similar
function as God's wife,
in the Amarna religion,
part of this responsibility
would have been to
maintain a state of
perpetual arousal. Reliefs
show this and the praises
for her "joining with her
beauty in propitiating
the world with her sweet
voice and her fair hands
holding the vases for plums"

Nefertiti

gazing out at Thebes,
the Nile, a smooth
cobalt ribbon, lush
palms and orchids,
a thick green and
black soil. She is
calm and still
posing for the
sculptor who will
make her immortal.
He has studied
her, has almost
tasted her luscious
neck, amazing lips
he will paint and
remember redder than
any red lips
could be. Maybe she
is drifting in thoughts
of the newest baby
swelling beneath
her silk. She wears
gold nefer beads
she knows, even so
young, she will be
buried with. Is her
slight smile for
the painter? Has she
fantasy of his long
fingers on her skin?
Peacock feathers
catch the slight
breeze, sway in
vases etched with
ostriches, boats, and

geometrical designs.
The heat lulls like
a lover's touch. If only
this child is a boy.
She imagines statues
of him, hieroglyphs
of his name in
elaborate underground
burial chambers. But
for now, these sprawling
temples can wait. She is
watching the beauty
of her long swan neck
emerge from stone, feels
her body, lush as the land-
scape, lapis, gold and
ivory circling her tawny
skin, like the world
that loves her

Hours Posing for the Sculpture

her skin damp in
the hot Egyptian light,
her breasts pushed
against silk and
necklaces of gold and
Egyptian frieze glass.
Her daughter's
laughter in the
distance, slap of the
Nile on a blue boat.
Does she remember a
mother who called
her *Darling*? A
bride before 15, and
then her first child when
she was still one. Now,
in a bracelet of
young girls and the
king's love, like a flower
that keeps unfolding,
her body glows like her
eyes and smile; her
skin can barely
keep her inside

Nefertiti Posing Hours with the Nile as a Backdrop

she could smell sun
on her skin. Hours
gazing into the
distance. Maybe a
favorite cat's fur
rubbed her tawny
skin. A daughter
singing in the
distance, maybe
playing a lute in the
shade of the date
tree. Those hours,
sitting so quietly.
Did she wonder
how her likeness
would be used?
In a temple or
tomb? Or on some
textile? Would it
be wrapped in her
mummy folds
with amulets and
beads? And if she
lived past her beauty,
would she be
discarded? Maybe
abandoned if the
new baby swelling
under her silk wasn't
a boy? I think of
her in the papyrus
and barley wind,
in the glow of

her king's love and
honor, a woman
with power, not just
the most worshipped
and beautiful
and loved as she
hopes she will be in
the afterlife if
nothing goes wrong

Afternoons, Alone in the Temple for Hours

I imagine Nefertiti thinking
of what she'd want in the
rooms of her last home,
in her temples and tombs,
can picture her planning
carved and brightly painted
beams and of course the
sun would be at the perfect
angle so it would rise in
the morning and pass over
the entrance to the temple.
She would want a tomb fit
for gods, painted decorations
of the cosmos and after-
life, pottery vessels and gold
furniture. For her pleasure
in this life, epic stories
about wandering heroes,
tales of pharaohs, magicians,
books on etiquette, and comic
stories about deities. The
Egyptians wrote political
propaganda, what may have
been the world's first fairy
tales. Nefertiti must have loved
the seductive love poetry,
dramas, and would have smiled
thinking about the performances
that accompanied some burials.
And tho' no music survives, I can
imagine her fingers stroking
musical instruments included
in several burials and depicted
on walls of the tombs, and singing
a little lullaby she can imagine
harps and flutes singing to
her for this last sleep

Nefertiti on a Night She Couldn't Sleep

listening to night
birds on the Nile.
Wind in the barley.
Stars like glow
lights in the sand.
Gold and white
camellias. Amethyst
at her fingertips.
Someone to play
the lute. Someone
to sing to her six
children. Feldspar
and galena for
cosmetics, her
husband for love
and power, some-
one to keep her
safe, and her beauty
like a cape of
jewels no one
could buy or trade
in Canaan, Syria,
or Mesopotamia
for this moment,
this time

Sitting on Her Husband's Knees

maybe whispering his
name, bird names, the
names of flowers.
Look, her long swan
neck, gorgeous as
any goddess. And
those cheekbones,
glistening. She made
her own creams
from the Galena
plants in the garden.
Behind those
huge eyes, names of
spells and hexes,
names of children
coiled in her dreams.
Children with her
hypnotic eyes,
children who would
rule, and in their
last hours, call
her name out across
the desert

When I Read How King Akhenaten's

love for Nefertiti is seen
in hieroglyphs at Amara.
"Fair of face," he says,
and adorned with double
plumes. I think of how
he must have dreamt of
holding her, called her
love names of course in
reality he never could.
Delicious names, too
secret, maybe the names
of flowers that only open
in the East. Maybe he
thought of her in darkness,
could almost smell her
hair, shudder at all
the men wild to
hold her

Did the King Shudder, Knowing How Many Men Wanted Her

Did he imagine other
tongues on her lips?
Their kisses falling
over her perfect
body like stars?

But, instead, knelt
before her and wrote
of how the king
rejoices at her

voice, how he
hopes she may
live forever
and always

Nefertiti as America's Top Model

I think of her trying
to win that spot, be
on the cover of
Seventeen and win
a Cover Girl contract.
When Bill Clinton
said he'd like to
ask the Peruvian
Ice Mummy out for
lunch, shouldn't
Nefertiti, with her
gorgeous skin,
beautifully bronze
as Tyra Banks's,
and even sharing
Tyra's so enormous,
stunning, magic eyes,
do as well? Name
another beauty who
has riveted so
many thru time.
Her long, slender neck,
lips more haunting,
more luscious
than Mona Lisa's.
You know she
would follow the
rules, would
not fight with the
other girls, but
keep her dignity. Her
long legs and
small breasts, her
knack for high
fashion, and she has

her own gorgeous
jewels. How could
Tyra, how could
any of the judges resist
her lustrous hair,
sun-touched
or frizzed, and who
would not kill for
her cheekbones?

Nefertiti

I think of Nefertiti
in her bracelet of
six girls. Who'd
imagine her
striking a female
captive on a royal
barge? She looks
so motherly. Her
long swan neck
seems made for
gold bracelets and
babies' arms.
Think of her in
her mortar-shaped
cap, her leonine
aspect, cat-like
as a sphinx, a mauve
sky behind her.
Her girls, a
sea of love. The
name for a boy child
like an animal
that won't sleep

Nefertiti

beautiful as Isis.
The king chose her
image to be engraved
in the 4 corners of
his sarcophagus to
protect his mummy

Carvings show them
kissing in a braid of
their daughters. You
can imagine each of
them praying to keep
the others safe, even

as corn bloomed in
the desert, shadows
rose as her cheek-
bones, and sadness
seemed so far away

Nefertiti

I think of her long bones,
enormous dark lake
eyes, that she would be
a beautiful ballerina,
pale, with that long
swan neck. You can't
imagine her not having
beautiful, perfect fingers.
Were there days, looking
out at the flood plain,
the rich black soil
and the Nile rapids,
she imagined herself free
as the sparkling water
under the blue, cloudless
sky, her feet tracing
hieroglyphs, a last
SOS?

While She Poses

in a gold chair like
a throne, days at
the window, her face
illuminated, her
eyes illuminating,
does she know she
will appear in twice
as many scenes as
her husband? Or
that, years after she
is the flesh and full-
lipped beauty gazing
as farmers pick flax
and barley, papyrus,
and melons and she
strokes a cat with eyes
as huge and almond-
shaped as hers that
rubs against her
tawny skin, nothing
will be as she dreams.
She will always
be *the beautiful
one,* and because
so little is known
about her, the world
will be starved
for more

Nefertiti

in images, a fertility
symbol, often with
her six daughters.
She wears the same
fashions as images
of the gods. From
the palace, little
boats with sails
flutter like flower
petals. Does she
imagine escaping?
Imagine life far from
this new capital?
The king at her side,
the smell of the Nile.
So much beginning.
Akhenaten, dedicated
to the royal couple's
new religion where
she would reign,
strong and powerful,
startlingly, in her
new tight-clinging
robe tied with a red
sash, with the ends
hanging in front.
Did she worry, fear
her beauty fading?
That she might
lose the hypnotic
power she held?
Or did she luxuriate
in her Nubian wig,
plaited with a queen's
strands, secured by

a diadem, and then
the crown with
plumes on a disk.
Did she imagine
nights she would
call out her
new daughter's
name like a pain cry,
a tombstone she
would not
say again?

Think of Nefertiti

too beautiful to
describe. Her name,
for years, chiseled off
monuments, her face
defaced on statues,
her city razed to
earth, its bricks
stolen and carried
off like burned
manuscripts. Think
how those chisels were
not able to disfigure
everything, how
border stelae in remote
areas survived the
destructive fury.
Clay tablet letters
written to foreign
capitals also escaped
the censor's knife,
and archaeologists began
to read these scattered
messages and filled
in the empty spaces on
monuments in Thebes and
Karnak. Today, Akhenaten
is considered one of the
most remarkable
personalities, a man ahead
of his time. And
Nefertiti, was she
as beautiful as the epithets
claimed? Did she share
his vision? I think of
the first person to

lay eyes on Nefertiti's face
in 3,300 years. On Dec.
6, 1912, he was digging in
a garden when the rays
of sun lit up the gold
and blue colors of
the queen's necklace. A
shout brought all picks
and shovels to a standstill.
One professor was sent
for from his makeshift
hut where he slept
after his midday meal.
The statue lay buried,
head down, in the debris.
Once uncovered, the
sandstone figure
was in near-perfect
condition. The only
visible damage is the
chipped earlobes
and the inlay of the retina
of the left eye that was
missing. As to her beauty:
it is timeless

Why, Maybe, There is a Flaw in the Gorgeous Bust of Nefertiti

the startling eyes and face,
but I think of how, when
pulled out of dirt and mud,
her earlobes were chipped,
the retina of the left eye
was missing. I think of the
dirt she was found in, sifted
again and again thru fine
and finer mesh, how all
the ear pieces were found,
but the eye inlay was
never recovered. Later
examination revealed it was
never inserted. Some say
the artist was interrupted
at his work and left the
workshop and took the
inlay with him, never to
return. Or that the
artist had fallen in love
with the queen as she posed
for him, was jilted by her
and, in an impotent rage,
refused to complete
his masterwork. Some
say this is not as
far-fetched as it seems;
the queen was known
to be flirtatious. Another
theory is that Nefertiti
had gone blind in one eye
and the artist
had opted for realism

over dignity. Still, the grace-
ful curve of her long neck,
the arched eyebrow,
and the hint of a smile on
the queen's sensual lips
are nothing like the ice-glare
of traditional Egyptian
statues

Those Days Posing for the Artist

pyramids in the distance.
Did Nefertiti ever dream
of her last home in the
plush death cave with
gold and jasper and
jasmine burning? How
could anyone whose
beauty captured all the
breath, the attention, in
Thebes not dream it
wouldn't always? That
life-like beauty radiating
from that bust of lime-
stone and plaster
must have made her
wonder what else when
it was gone. She must
have daydreamed
hours in the hot Egyptian
afternoons as flowers
that bloomed only once
in a lifetime opened
and closed. I think of the
hands stroking and
chipping at the plaster,
imagining what he pulled
into a life that would
go on forever was
the warm body so near
him as he smoothed a soft
brown color on the face
and neck of the bust,
as close to skin
as he could make it, and
painted her lips so

calm and red, making the
mouth soft, sensuous;
then outlining eyebrows
and eyes with black.
Then he painted
her hair a blue, rich as the
Nile, giving her the wildest
power and beauty of
rainforests, with
painted jewelry in
her hair and around that
gorgeous neck; blue,
green, and gold,
exotic, entrancing,
something no
one has a name for

How Nefertiti Got Her Blue-Black Hair and Disappeared

in one story, when
the purple sky was
going ink, blackness
crept over bundles
of garlic and roast
duck on a night the
donkeys were bray-
ing. The night was
still. The stars, a
glaze of rhinestones
over its skin. Tho'
Nefertiti thinks of
her silks and gold,
her broaches and
wigs studded with
diamonds, she pulls
on, long before the
first sliver of light,
a man's clothes and
goes on to rule under
the name *Smenkhkare*

In One Shrine

Nefertiti is holding one daughter
while the king kisses her and
the little girl, Meritaten, plays
on her mother's lap, gazes up
lovingly. Ankhesenpaaten, the
smallest, sits on Nefertiti's
shoulder and fiddles with her
earring. Think of Nefertiti in
this brief moment in their lives,
caught in an act of mutual
affection. Think how mysterious,
no son was shown in any reliefs
tho' the daughter's names are
chiseled: Meritaten, 1356 BC;
Meketaten and Ankhesenpaaten,
1349 BC; Neferneferuaten,
1344 BC; Neferneferure, 1341 BC;
and Setepenre, 1339 BC, and
then the official family, with all
of Nefertiti's daughters, and then in
1936 Meketaten died in child-
birth. After 1335, Nefertiti seemed
to vanish. There is no trace of
her tomb. Some jewelry bearing
the cartouche was found outside
the royal tomb at Akhetaten.
No one knows if she died, was
murdered, went away in disguise.
The end of her life as mysterious
as her birth, blood, her
half-smile

Another Dead End

in 2003, a specialist in
ancient hair announced
Nerfertiti's tomb may
have been found, that
maybe she was really
the Pharaoh Smenkhkare.
The mummy, examined
by scans, was discovered
damaged in a way that
suggested the body had
been desecrated either
at the time of death or
soon after. Mummification
techniques, such as the
use of embalming fluid
and the presence of an
intact brain, suggest
a royal mummy. The age
of the body, the presence
of embedded nefer beads,
the fact that the arm had
been buried in the position
reserved for pharaohs
and had been snapped off
by vandals and replaced
with another arm in a normal
position, and a wig, a unique
style worn by Nefertiti,
all seemed clues. But later,
the head of Egypt's Council
for Antiquities dismissed the
claim: not enough evidence.
And a month or two later,
the one in charge of the
exploration said, "I'm sure
this mummy is not a female."

The Beautiful One Has Come

and left mysteriously,
as with her birth.
So many coffins, but
no sign of Nefertiti,
no sign of the six
princesses she bore.
In one tomb, many
ceramic jars and
several wooden
coffins with yellow
painted faces, but
no mummies. But
in the eyes of the
painted faces, a link
to Nefertiti, whose
name means *the
beautiful one has
come*. No one knows
who the coffins are
for, but the eyes are
exotic. If not a royal
tomb, what? Seven
coffins, a small gilt
coffinette, two large
alabaster vessels,
floral garlands,
pillows, natron, the
natural salt used in
mummification, and
many ceramics,
fragments of gold,
eerie, mysterious as
a song there are
no words for

Acknowledgments

Some of the poems in this book appeared in the following journals:

2 Bridges Review

Assisi: An Online Journal of Arts & Letters

Erzsebet

ESP Press

Harpur Palate

Pirene's Fountain

Soundings Review

The South Carolina Review

Tales of the Talisman

Winterhawk

About the Author

Lyn Lifshin has published over 130 books and chapbooks, including three from Black Sparrow Press: *Cold Comfort, Before It's Light,* and *Another Woman Who Looks Like Me*. Before writing *Secretariat: The Red Freak, The Miracle,* Lifshin wrote her prize-winning book about the short-lived, beautiful racehorse Ruffian: *The Licorice Daughter: My Year With Ruffian*. She also wrote *Barbaro: Beyond Brokenness*. Recent books include *Ballroom*; *All the Poets Who Have Touched Me, Living and Dead*; *All True, Especially The Lies*; *Light At the End: The Jesus Poems*; *Katrina*; *In Mirrors*; *Persephone*; *Lost In The Fog*; and *Knife Edge & Absinthe: The Tango Poems*. NYQ Books published *A Girl Goes into The Woods*. Also just out: *For the Roses: Poems Inspired by Joni Mitchell*; *Hitchcock Hotel*, from Danse Macabre; *Tangled as the Alphabet: The Turkey Poems*, from Night Ballet Press; and *Malala. The Marilyn Poems* was just released from Rubber Boots Press. An update to her Gale Research Autobiography is also out: *Lips, Blues, Blue Lace: On The Outside*. Also just out is a DVD of the documentary film about her: *Lyn Lifshin: Not Made Of Glass*. Forthcoming books include *Moving Through Stained Glass: the Maple Poems*.

Learn more about Lyn Lifshin at her website: www.lynlifshin.com.

GLASS LYRE PRESS, LLC
"Exceptional works to replenish the spirit"

Poetry collections
Poetry chapbooks
Select short & flash fiction
Anthologies

Glass Lyre Press is a small independent literary press interested in work which is technically accomplished and distinctive in style, as well as fresh in its approach and treatment. Glass Lyre seeks writers of diverse backgrounds who display mastery over the many areas of contemporary literature: writers with a powerful and dynamic aesthetic, and ability to stir the imagination and engage the emotions and intellect of a wide audience of readers.

The Glass Lyre vision is to connect the world through language and art. We hope to expand the scope of poetry and short fiction for the general reader through exceptionally well-written books, which call forth our deepest emotions and thoughts, delight our senses, challenge our minds, and provide clarity, resonance and insight.

www.GlassLyrePress.com

www.ingramcontent.com/pod-product-compliance
Lightning Source LLC
Chambersburg PA
CBHW020657300426
44112CB00007B/417